Please Don't Move My Grandma's Chair

A Children's Story About Grief and the Hope of Heaven.

Rev. Cheryl Kincaid

To my Grandmother, Helen Mix.

Daddy, please don't move Grandma's chair, the one with roses and pears.

The chair where she gently rocked me whenever she held me near.

She placed her seat by the fire to keep her right side warm.

She held me on her left side to keep me safe from harm.

Please don't take Grandma's chair, the one that's tattered and old.

She used to sing me songs in that chair while she counted my fingers and toes.

Please don't take Grandma's chair, the one that smells like her perfume.

It doesn't belong to any place but here, in Grandma's favorite room.

Daddy sighed and wiped away the tears.

"It is a good chair, but Grandma is no longer here.

"I sat with her in that chair when I was small, like you.

We laughed about inside jokes, and sometimes we cried,

too.

She would sit in that chair and smile when I made her proud.

And sternly sit up with a frown when I played music too loud.

I hate to say goodbye to this chair, this strong old chair that creeks at night.

But Grandma got sick and so tired, so she whispered to me one night.

'I want to be with Jesus,' she told me with a smile and a sigh.

So I held her close, and we both said goodbye.

"I know you miss your grandma sitting here, smiling by the fire.

But now she's in heaven, and she is no longer tired.

But she left us many things when she told us goodbye

She left us her love, her wisdom, and memories."

Then I took Daddy's hand and said, "She left me her lullabies."

Daddy and Brother moved the chair to the curb outside.

While Mommy held me on her lap and whispered, "It's

okay to cry."

The next morning, I saw a lady standing outside my yard.

She leaned back and rubbed her round belly while smiling

at the man in a car.

"We need a rocking chair for our nursery," she said, "and

this one could be ours.

It just needs a little mending and stuffing in the seat.

The pears and roses against the nursery wall would look

rather sweet."

"It could fit inside our truck," the man said, "and I could

tie it tight,

With the roses and pears in our nursery, it would be just

right."

So I watched them take the chair, the one that made me

cry.

As I pushed open the screen, I shouted before their truck

drove by.

"It's a good old chair that will help you snuggle at night.

It was my grandma's chair, and it is especially good for lullabies."

About the Author

Reverend Cheryl Kincaid is a Presbyterian Minister who studied Marriage and Family Therapy at Bethel and has a Master of Divinity from San Francisco Theological Seminary. Rev. Kincaid facilitated support groups for women who had suffered abuse for seven years and has worked in group homes.

Rev. Kincaid seeks to tell the story of God's comforting redemptive grace amid an imperfect world. Rev. Cheryl Kincaid has twenty years of experience in Christian ministry, and she confesses that many of her stories were inspired from witnessing God's redemptive grace unfold in wounded Christian's lives, including her own. She is the author of six books: *Hearing the Gospel through Charles Dickens' A Christmas Carol, The Little Clay Pot, The Little Candle that Was Frightened of the Dark, Karrie's Thorn and A Forgotten Door Called Home.*

To learn more about Reverend Kincaid's books and biography please visit: https://revcherylkincaid.com